# Russian and Ukraine War:The potential for escalation and the risk of wider regional conflict.

## By

## Egor Lavrentiev

# Content

## Introduction

The situation between Russia and Ukraine is complex and fraught with tension, and there is a risk that it could escalate into a wider regional conflict or even a world war. The conflict has its roots in a long-standing dispute over the Crimean Peninsula, which was annexed by Russia in 2014. Since then, fighting has continued in eastern Ukraine, with pro-Russian separatists battling Ukrainian government forces.

The potential for escalation of this conflict is high. Both sides have been building up their military capabilities, and there have been reports of increased troop movements and military exercises. There is also the risk of miscalculation or accidental escalation, particularly if either side misinterprets the other's intentions.

If the conflict were to escalate, it could draw in other countries in the region and potentially even the wider international community. NATO has expressed support for Ukraine, and if Russian forces were to invade Ukraine, it is possible that NATO could become involved in the conflict. Russia, in turn, has warned that any NATO presence in Ukraine would be seen as a provocation.

There are also concerns about the potential use of nuclear weapons. Both Russia and Ukraine possess nuclear weapons, and there have been reports of increased activity at nuclear facilities in both countries. The use of nuclear weapons would have devastating consequences, not just for the countries involved but for the entire world.

Open sidebar

Russian-Ukraine Conflict Risk.

The ongoing conflict between Russia and Ukraine has been a source of concern for the international community, with potential for escalation and the risk of wider regional conflict. The conflict has its roots in the historical and cultural ties between the two countries, as well as in geopolitical tensions and competing interests in the region. Since 2014, Russia has annexed Crimea and supported separatist rebels in eastern Ukraine, leading to a deadly and protracted conflict that has claimed thousands of lives and displaced millions of people. The conflict has also strained relations between Russia and the West, with sanctions and diplomatic measures imposed by both sides. Despite efforts to negotiate a peaceful resolution, the conflict remains unresolved, and the potential for further escalation and wider regional conflict remains a significant concern. This paper will examine the key factors driving the conflict, the potential for escalation, and the risk of wider regional conflict, as well as the implications for the international community.

In summary, the situation between Russia and Ukraine is a cause for concern, and there is a risk that it could escalate into a wider regional conflict or even a world war. It is important for all parties to engage in dialogue and work towards a peaceful resolution to the conflict.

Historical Background of Conflict on Russian and Ukraine war

The conflict between Russia and Ukraine began in 2014 when Ukraine's pro-Russian President, Viktor Yanukovych, was overthrown by a popular uprising. Russia annexed Crimea, a Ukrainian territory, and began supporting separatists in the eastern Ukrainian regions of Donetsk and Luhansk.

The roots of the conflict date back to the dissolution of the Soviet Union in 1991, when Ukraine became an independent nation. Ukraine has always been a strategic buffer between Russia and the West, and its political orientation has been a subject of debate since independence.

The conflict escalated in 2014 when Yanukovych's ouster led to a pro-Western government coming to power in Ukraine. Russia viewed this as a threat to its national security and began supporting separatists in eastern Ukraine, who declared their independence and formed the self-proclaimed Donetsk and Luhansk People's Republics.

The conflict has since claimed over 13,000 lives and displaced over 1.6 million people. It has also had a significant impact on the global political landscape, with Russia's annexation of Crimea leading to international condemnation and sanctions.

Efforts to resolve the conflict through diplomacy have been ongoing, with several ceasefires agreed upon but ultimately broken. The Minsk agreements, signed in 2015, aimed to establish a lasting peace but have yet to be fully implemented.

The conflict has also had implications for the broader geopolitical landscape, with Russia's actions leading to increased tensions with the West. The conflict in Ukraine has become a focal point in the ongoing debate over Russia's intentions and its relationship with the rest of the world.

Current Situation and Tensions on Ukraine and Russian War

The situation in Ukraine has been tense for several years now, particularly due to the ongoing conflict between Ukraine and Russia. This conflict started in 2014 when Russia annexed Crimea, a Ukrainian territory, and began supporting separatist rebels in the Donetsk and Luhansk regions of Ukraine. Since then, there have been sporadic outbreaks of fighting in these regions, with both sides accusing each other of violating ceasefires and escalating the conflict.

The war has caused significant humanitarian suffering, with thousands of people killed and many more displaced from their homes. It has also strained relations between Russia and Western countries, who have imposed economic sanctions on Russia in response to its actions in Ukraine.

In recent months, tensions have escalated again as Russia has built up its military presence along the border with Ukraine. Western countries have expressed concern over this buildup, with some officials warning that Russia may be planning a new offensive in Ukraine. Ukrainian officials have also raised the alarm, accusing Russia of amassing tens of thousands of troops near the border.

The situation remains fluid and unpredictable, with both sides engaging in military maneuvers and rhetoric that could lead to further escalation. The international community has called for restraint and a peaceful resolution to the conflict, but the deep-rooted tensions between Ukraine and Russia make this a difficult task.

In summary, the conflict between Ukraine and Russia remains a significant source of tension and instability in the region. The buildup of military forces and rhetoric from both sides has raised concerns about the possibility of renewed violence and further humanitarian suffering. A peaceful resolution to the conflict remains elusive, and the international community continues to monitor the situation closely.

## Military Buildup and Troop Movements on Ukraine and Russian war

In recent years, there have been tensions between Ukraine and Russia, and the situation has escalated with military buildup and troop movements. The conflict dates back to 2014, when Russia annexed Crimea from Ukraine, leading to a military conflict in eastern Ukraine that has been ongoing ever since.

In recent months, both Ukraine and Russia have been increasing their military presence in the region, with troop movements and military exercises taking place on both sides. The buildup has raised concerns among the international community, with many fearing that it could lead to a wider conflict.

Russia has been accused of amassing troops and military hardware along the border with Ukraine, with reports suggesting that as many as 100,000 Russian troops may be stationed in the region. In response, Ukraine has also been increasing its military presence in the area, with reports of troops and equipment being moved to the frontlines.

The situation has been further complicated by the presence of separatist groups in eastern Ukraine, who are believed to be backed by Russia. These groups have been involved in sporadic fighting with Ukrainian government forces, and the increased military buildup has raised fears that the conflict could escalate.

The international community has been closely monitoring the situation, with many calling for a de-escalation of tensions. The United States and other NATO countries have expressed support for Ukraine, and have called on Russia to respect Ukraine's territorial integrity and sovereignty.

Despite the calls for de-escalation, the situation on the ground remains tense, and there are fears that the conflict could escalate into a wider war. The situation in Ukraine and Russia is a reminder of the ongoing challenges facing the international community in dealing with conflicts and tensions around the world.

## Risk of Miscalculation and Accidental Escalation on Russian and Ukraine War

The ongoing conflict between Russia and Ukraine has been a cause of concern for the international community, as the risk of miscalculation and accidental escalation remains high. The conflict began in 2014, when Russia annexed Crimea and supported separatists in eastern Ukraine. Since then, there have been sporadic clashes, with both sides accusing the other of aggression.

One of the main risks of miscalculation in this conflict is the lack of communication and trust between the two sides. The absence of diplomatic channels has led to misunderstandings and misinterpretations of each other's actions, which could trigger a military response. This was evident in 2018 when Russia captured three Ukrainian naval vessels in the Kerch Strait, leading to a sharp escalation of tensions.

Another risk is the involvement of third parties. Ukraine has received military support from the United States and other Western countries, while Russia has close ties with Belarus, which borders Ukraine. Any actions by these countries could escalate the conflict beyond the control of the two sides, leading to a wider conflict.

The use of military force also poses a significant risk of escalation. Both Russia and Ukraine have significant military capabilities, including nuclear weapons. Any use of force, intentional or accidental, could have catastrophic consequences not only for the two countries but also for the entire world.

The conflict has also raised concerns about cyberattacks and disinformation campaigns. Both sides have been accused of using these tactics to spread false information and undermine the other's position. A successful cyberattack or disinformation campaign could cause significant damage and lead to a military response.

In conclusion, the risk of miscalculation and accidental escalation in the Russian and Ukrainian conflict remains high. The lack of communication and trust, involvement of third parties, use of military force, and cyberattacks are all factors that could trigger an escalation. It is essential for the two sides to engage in meaningful dialogue and for the international community to support efforts to resolve the conflict peacefully.

Possibility of NATO Involvement in Ukraine and Russian war

The possibility of NATO involvement in the ongoing conflict between Ukraine and Russia remains a topic of great debate and concern. While NATO has expressed support for Ukraine's sovereignty and territorial integrity, the alliance has not yet taken any military action against Russia.

The conflict in Ukraine began in 2014 when Russia annexed Crimea and began supporting separatist movements in eastern Ukraine. Since then, tensions between Ukraine and Russia have remained high, and there have been numerous ceasefire violations and military clashes.

NATO has provided political and economic support to Ukraine, including sanctions against Russia and the provision of military aid. However, the alliance has not committed to military intervention in the conflict.

There are several reasons for NATO's reluctance to intervene militarily in the conflict. One major concern is the risk of escalation and a direct military confrontation with Russia. Any military action by NATO could provoke a significant response from Russia, potentially leading to a larger conflict.

Another consideration is the lack of consensus among NATO members on the issue. While some member countries are pushing for a more aggressive stance towards Russia, others are more cautious and prefer to pursue diplomatic solutions.

Overall, while NATO's involvement in the conflict between Ukraine and Russia remains a possibility, it is not currently a likely scenario. The alliance is likely to continue providing political and economic support to Ukraine while pursuing diplomatic solutions to the conflict.

Concerns over Nuclear Weapons on Ukraine and Russia war.

The ongoing conflict between Ukraine and Russia has sparked concerns over the potential use of nuclear weapons. Both Ukraine and Russia are nuclear-armed nations, with Russia being one of the world's largest nuclear powers.

The fear is that the conflict could escalate to the point where one or both sides may consider using nuclear weapons, either as a preemptive measure or in response to an attack. The use of nuclear weapons would have catastrophic consequences not only for Ukraine and Russia but for the entire world.

One concern is that the conflict could lead to a nuclear arms race in the region. If Ukraine feels threatened by Russia's nuclear arsenal, it may feel the need to develop its own nuclear weapons as a deterrent. This, in turn, could prompt other neighboring countries to do the same, leading to a dangerous proliferation of nuclear weapons.

Another concern is the risk of accidental or unauthorized use of nuclear weapons. During times of heightened tensions, there is always a risk of miscommunication or misinterpretation of actions, which could lead to a nuclear launch. Additionally, the theft or unauthorized access to nuclear weapons by non-state actors, such as terrorist groups, could also result in a catastrophic event.

To prevent the use of nuclear weapons in the Ukraine-Russia conflict, the international community has called for diplomatic efforts to de-escalate the situation. It is crucial that both sides engage in constructive dialogue to find a

Potential Consequences of Wider Regional Conflict on Ukraine and Russian war leading to world war 3

The ongoing conflict between Ukraine and Russia has already caused significant tension and instability in the region. However, if the conflict were to escalate and result in a wider regional conflict, the potential consequences could be catastrophic and even lead to a global conflict.

Here are some of the potential consequences of a wider regional conflict in Ukraine:

Humanitarian Crisis: The conflict has already resulted in a significant humanitarian crisis, with thousands of people displaced and in need of aid. If the conflict were to escalate, the number of refugees and displaced people would increase, putting further strain on resources and exacerbating the humanitarian crisis.

Economic Fallout: Ukraine is a major transit country for natural gas pipelines from Russia to Europe, and any disruption in these pipelines would have a significant impact on the global energy market. In addition, a wider regional conflict would disrupt trade and investment, leading to economic instability in the region and beyond.

Military Escalation: If the conflict were to escalate, there is a risk of military escalation, with other countries getting involved in the conflict. This could lead to a wider regional conflict and even a global conflict.

Nuclear War: Russia has the world's largest nuclear arsenal, and any military escalation could potentially lead to the use of nuclear weapons. This would have catastrophic consequences, not only for the region but for the entire world.

Diplomatic Fallout: The conflict has already strained relations between Russia and the West, and a wider regional conflict could lead to further diplomatic fallout. This would make it more difficult to resolve the conflict through diplomatic means, potentially leading to further military escalation.Overall, the potential consequences of a wider regional conflict in Ukraine are significant and far-reaching. It is important for all parties to work towards a peaceful resolution to the conflict to avoid these catastrophic outcomes.

Importance of Dialogue and Peaceful between Russian and Ukraine to stop the war

The ongoing conflict between Russia and Ukraine has had a devastating impact on both countries and the wider region. The conflict has caused thousands of deaths and displaced millions of people. While there are many factors that have contributed to the conflict, the importance of dialogue and peaceful relations between Russia and Ukraine cannot be overstated.

Dialogue between Russia and Ukraine is crucial because it provides an opportunity for both sides to share their perspectives and concerns. Without dialogue, misunderstandings can persist and tensions can escalate. Dialogue can help to identify areas of common ground and areas of disagreement, which can then be addressed through negotiation and compromise.

Peaceful relations between Russia and Ukraine are also important because they provide a foundation for stability and security in the region. When countries have peaceful relations, they are more likely to cooperate on issues of mutual concern, such as economic development, energy security, and regional stability. This can lead to greater prosperity and security for both countries and the wider region.

Furthermore, dialogue and peaceful relations can help to build trust between Russia and Ukraine. Trust is essential for any long-term resolution of the conflict. Without trust, it is difficult to make progress on any issue, as each side may view the other with suspicion or hostility. Trust can be built through a process of incremental steps, such as the exchange of prisoners or the implementation of a ceasefire.

In conclusion, the importance of dialogue and peaceful relations between Russia and Ukraine cannot be overstated. Both countries must be willing to engage in dialogue and work towards a peaceful resolution of the conflict. This will require compromise and a willingness to see the other side's perspective. But if both sides are committed to dialogue and peace, it is possible to end the conflict and build a more stable and prosperous future for both countries and the wider region.

Allies to the Russian side

In 2014, Russia annexed Crimea, a region previously part of Ukraine, and this action has been widely condemned by the international community. Since then, there have been ongoing tensions between Russia and Ukraine, and in 2022, Russia launched a military offensive into Ukrainian territory, causing further escalation of the conflict.

In terms of allies, Russia has the support of some countries, such as Belarus, Kazakhstan, and Armenia. These countries have expressed their support for Russia's actions in Ukraine and have been criticized by other nations for their stance.

On the other hand, Ukraine has the support of many countries, including the United States, Canada, the United Kingdom, France, Germany, and many others. These countries have condemned Russia's actions and have provided Ukraine with diplomatic and military support, including sanctions on Russia and the provision of military aid to Ukraine.

It is important to note that the situation is complex, and alliances and opinions can change over time. It is crucial to follow reliable sources and stay informed about the latest developments in the ongoing conflict.

Ukraine-Russia Conflict Casualties

The conflict between Ukraine and Russia has been ongoing since 2014, when Russia annexed Crimea from Ukraine and began supporting separatist rebels in the Donbass region of eastern Ukraine. The conflict has resulted in a significant number of casualties on both sides.

According to the United Nations, as of January 2022, over 13,000 people have been killed in the conflict, including both military personnel and civilians. The majority of these casualties have occurred in the Donetsk and Luhansk regions of eastern Ukraine, where the fighting has been most intense.

The Ukrainian government has reported that over 3,000 Ukrainian soldiers have been killed in the conflict, with another 8,000 wounded. Civilian casualties have also been significant, with the Ukrainian government reporting over 7,000 civilian deaths and over 18,000 civilian injuries as a result of the conflict.

On the Russian side, casualty numbers are less clear, as the Russian government has not released official figures. However, it is believed that several hundred Russian soldiers have been killed in the conflict, either as part of the regular Russian military or as part of Russian-backed separatist groups. Additionally, there have been reports of Russian civilian casualties, although the number is difficult to verify.

The conflict has taken a significant toll on the civilian population in eastern Ukraine, with many people forced to flee their homes and seek refuge in other parts of the country. The conflict has also had a negative impact on the Ukrainian economy, with infrastructure and businesses in the affected regions severely damaged.

Efforts to find a resolution to the conflict have been ongoing, including peace talks and ceasefire agreements, but progress has been slow. The ongoing conflict and casualties serve as a reminder of the devastating impact that armed conflict can have on both military personnel and civilians alike.

Characters on Ukraine and Russian war

The conflict between Ukraine and Russia has involved a number of different characters, from political leaders and military officials to ordinary citizens caught in the crossfire. Here are some of the key players in this ongoing conflict:

Petro Poroshenko: Poroshenko was the President of Ukraine from 2014 to 2019, and played a key role in the country's response to Russian aggression. He implemented a number of reforms aimed at modernizing Ukraine and strengthening its military capabilities, and oversaw the launch of several offensives against Russian-backed separatists in eastern Ukraine.

Vladimir Putin: As the President of Russia, Putin has been a central figure in the conflict from the very beginning. He has repeatedly denied that Russian forces are involved in the fighting, despite overwhelming evidence to the contrary. Putin has also been accused of annexing Crimea in 2014 and providing military support to separatists in eastern Ukraine.

Volodymyr Zelensky: Zelensky is the current President of Ukraine, having taken office in 2019. He has vowed to continue fighting for Ukraine's territorial integrity and to negotiate a peaceful end to the conflict. However, his efforts have been complicated by ongoing violence and political instability in the region.

Alexander Zakharchenko: Zakharchenko was a prominent separatist leader in eastern Ukraine who was killed in a bombing in 2018. He was widely believed to have been backed by the Russian government, and his death sparked renewed fighting in the region.

Sergei Shoigu: Shoigu is the Minister of Defense of the Russian Federation, and has played a key role in directing Russian military operations in Ukraine. He has been accused of overseeing the deployment of Russian troops and weapons to separatist forces in the east.

Nadiya Savchenko: Savchenko is a Ukrainian military pilot who was captured by separatist forces in 2014 and held in a Russian prison for over two years. She was eventually released in a prisoner exchange, and has become a vocal critic of both the Ukrainian and Russian governments.

Donetsk People's Republic: The Donetsk People's Republic is a separatist group that controls a large swath of territory in eastern Ukraine. They have been accused of numerous human rights violations, and are widely believed to receive support from the Russian government.

Ukrainian civilians: Perhaps the most tragic figures in the conflict are the millions of Ukrainian civilians who have been affected by the fighting. Many have been forced to flee their homes, and countless others have been killed or injured in the violence. Their stories serve as a reminder of the human cost of war, and the urgent need for a peaceful resolution to this conflict.

Resolution on Russian and Ukraine war

The conflict between Russia and Ukraine began in 2014 when Russia annexed Crimea, a Ukrainian territory. The conflict has escalated into a full-scale war in eastern Ukraine, where Russian-backed separatists have been fighting Ukrainian government forces. Despite several ceasefire agreements, the conflict has continued, with sporadic fighting and casualties reported regularly.

International efforts to resolve the conflict have been ongoing, including diplomatic negotiations, sanctions, and peace talks. However, a lasting solution has not yet been achieved, and tensions between the two countries remain high.

In recent years, there have been some positive developments in the conflict. In July 2020, Ukraine and Russia exchanged a number of prisoners, including high-profile figures, as part of an agreement to ease tensions. In

February 2021, the two sides agreed to a ceasefire in eastern Ukraine, although violations of the ceasefire have been reported since then.

There have also been calls for a diplomatic solution to the conflict, with the United States and European Union urging Russia to withdraw its troops from eastern Ukraine and engage in dialogue with Ukraine to find a peaceful solution.

The resolution on the Russian and Ukraine war remains unclear. It is possible that a diplomatic solution may be reached through negotiations, although this will require compromise and concessions from both sides. It is also possible that the conflict may continue, with sporadic fighting and tensions remaining high. Ultimately, only time will tell what the resolution of the conflict will be.

Peace Efforts in Russia-Ukraine

The conflict between Russia and Ukraine has been ongoing since 2014, and has resulted in the loss of thousands of lives and displacement of millions of people. However, recent developments suggest that the two countries may be moving towards a resolution. Vladimir Putin, the President of Russia, and Volodymyr Zelensky, the President of Ukraine, have been working towards ending the war.

There are several causes behind the recent efforts to end the conflict. One of the main reasons is the economic impact of the war on both countries. The sanctions imposed on Russia by the West have had a significant impact on the Russian economy, and Ukraine has also suffered economically as a result of the conflict. Both countries recognize that ending the war would help to improve their economic situation.

Another cause of the recent peace efforts is the change in leadership in Ukraine. Volodymyr Zelensky was elected in 2019 on a platform of ending the war and achieving peace with

Russia. He has been willing to engage in dialogue with Putin, and has taken steps to reduce tensions between the two countries. Zelensky has also demonstrated a willingness to make concessions, such as agreeing to hold local elections in the disputed areas of Donbas, in order to reach a peace agreement.

On the other side, Vladimir Putin has also shown a willingness to negotiate. The conflict in Ukraine has been a significant drain on Russia's resources, and Putin has recognized that it is in Russia's best interests to find a peaceful resolution. Putin has also recognized that the conflict in Ukraine has damaged Russia's reputation on the world stage, and ending the conflict could help to improve Russia's image.

Despite the recent efforts to end the war, there are still significant obstacles to achieving peace. The conflict has been fueled by deep-seated historical and cultural differences between Russia and Ukraine, and there is a lack of trust between the two sides.

Additionally, there are powerful forces within both countries that oppose a peaceful resolution to the conflict. However, the fact that both Putin and Zelensky have expressed a desire for peace is a positive sign, and provides hope that a resolution may be possible in the near future.

Path to End Ukraine War

The ongoing conflict between Russia and Ukraine has been a source of tension and instability in the region for several years. The conflict began in 2014 when Russia annexed Crimea, a territory previously belonging to Ukraine. Since then, fighting has erupted in the eastern region of Ukraine, with separatist groups seeking to break away from the Ukrainian government and align with Russia.

To find a way forward on this conflict, it is essential to understand the root causes and the complex geopolitical landscape surrounding the issue. There are several steps that the international community can take to promote peace and stability in the region.

Firstly, diplomatic efforts must be intensified to resolve the conflict. The international community, including the United Nations and the European Union, must work together to bring the parties to the negotiating table. It is essential to ensure that all parties feel represented in the peace talks and that their concerns are addressed.

Secondly, both Russia and Ukraine must take concrete steps to de-escalate the situation on the ground. This includes a cessation of hostilities, the withdrawal of troops from the conflict zone, and the release of prisoners of war. The international community can play a crucial role in facilitating such measures, including the deployment of peacekeeping forces to monitor the situation.

Thirdly, efforts must be made to address the underlying issues that have fueled the conflict.

This includes addressing economic grievances, promoting greater autonomy for the regions, and protecting the rights of ethnic minorities. There must be a concerted effort to address these issues in a way that is inclusive, transparent, and fair to all parties.

Fourthly, the international community must ensure that humanitarian assistance reaches those affected by the conflict. Millions of people have been displaced, and there have been significant human rights violations on both sides of the conflict. Ensuring that aid reaches those in need is essential to alleviate suffering and build trust between the parties.

Finally, it is essential to ensure that any agreement reached is sustainable and enforceable. The international community must commit to providing the necessary resources and support to ensure that any peace agreement is successful. This includes financial assistance to rebuild infrastructure, support for economic development, and the establishment of a mechanism to monitor compliance with the agreement.

In conclusion, the conflict between Russia and Ukraine is a complex issue that requires a multifaceted approach to resolve. Diplomatic efforts must be intensified, both parties must take steps to de-escalate the situation, underlying issues must be addressed, humanitarian assistance must reach those in need, and any agreement must be sustainable and enforceable. By working together, the international community can promote peace and stability in the region and ensure that the people of Ukraine and Russia can live in peace and prosperity.

Conclusion.

The situation between Russia and Ukraine is complex, with historical, political, and economic factors contributing to the tensions.

The annexation of Crimea by Russia and the ongoing conflict in eastern Ukraine have strained relations between the two nations. The possibility of further escalation of the conflict, including the involvement of other nations in the region, cannot be ruled out.

It is essential to recognize the need for diplomacy and dialogue to resolve the situation peacefully. The international community has a critical role to play in facilitating discussions between the parties involved and preventing the conflict from escalating further.

In conclusion, the situation between Russia and Ukraine remains tense, and the potential for escalation and the risk of wider regional conflict cannot be ignored. It is crucial to focus on finding peaceful solutions to the conflict and promoting dialogue between the parties involved. The international community must work together to prevent any further escalation of the conflict and ensure stability in the region.

www.ingramcontent.com/pod-product-compliance
Lightning Source LLC
Chambersburg PA
CBHW071121220526
45467CB00004B/1996